Sacred Mountain
EVEREST

To Ken, Alexis, and Olivia—for demonstrating infinite patience throughout this process.
For Mom and Dad, who taught me that education is the key to life.
And above all, to the Sherpa, who give more to the world than they receive in return.
May Chomolungma always remain a unique and sacred place for generations to come.
—C.T.-B.

LEE & LOW BOOKS Inc., 95 Madison Avenue, New York, NY 10016
leeandlow.com
Manufactured in Singapore
Developed by Color-Bridge Books, LLC
Book design by Paul Colin, Cezanne Studio
Book production by The Kids at Our House
Photograph credits are located on page 48
The text is set in Sabon
10 9 8 7 6 5 4 3 2 1
First Edition
Library of Congress Cataloging-in-Publication Data
Taylor-Butler, Christine.
Sacred mountain : Everest / by Christine Taylor-Butler. — 1st ed.
p. cm.
Summary: "A cultural, geological, and ecological history of Mount Everest focusing on the indigenous Sherpa and their
spiritual connection to the mountain, record-setting multinational climbing expeditions, and the effects of tourism on
the environment. Illustrated with photographs, maps, diagrams, and timelines"—Provided by publisher.
ISBN 978-1-60060-255-9
1. Everest, Mount (China and Nepal)—Juvenile literature. 2. Sherpa (Nepalese people)—Juvenile literature.
3. Mountaineering—Everest, Mount (China and Nepal)—History—Juvenile literature. I. Title.
DS495.8.E9T39 2009
954.96—dc22   2008030423

Sacred Mountain
EVEREST

by Christine Taylor-Butler

LEE & LOW BOOKS Inc.
New York

On the border between Nepal and Tibet lies a mountain of unparalleled beauty and immense power. Shrouded in mystery, it stands highest among the Himalaya mountain peaks—the tallest mountain on Earth.

A sacred place, the mountain is home to the gods and goddesses worshipped by the native peoples who live in its shadow. For thousands of years, no man or woman dared to scale its heights. Today, those who take the risk ask for the mountain's blessing before climbing the icy slopes.

To the south, the people of Nepal call this majestic mountain Sagarmatha, Goddess of the Sky. To the north, the people of Tibet and China call it Chomolungma, Goddess Mother of the World. To the outside world, the mountain is known as Everest.

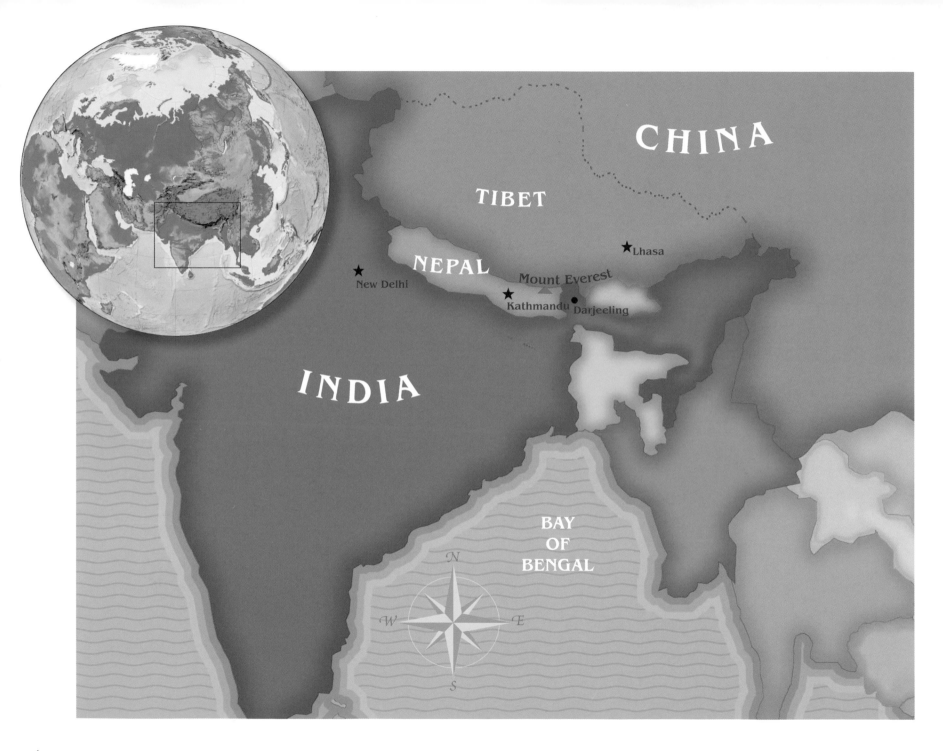

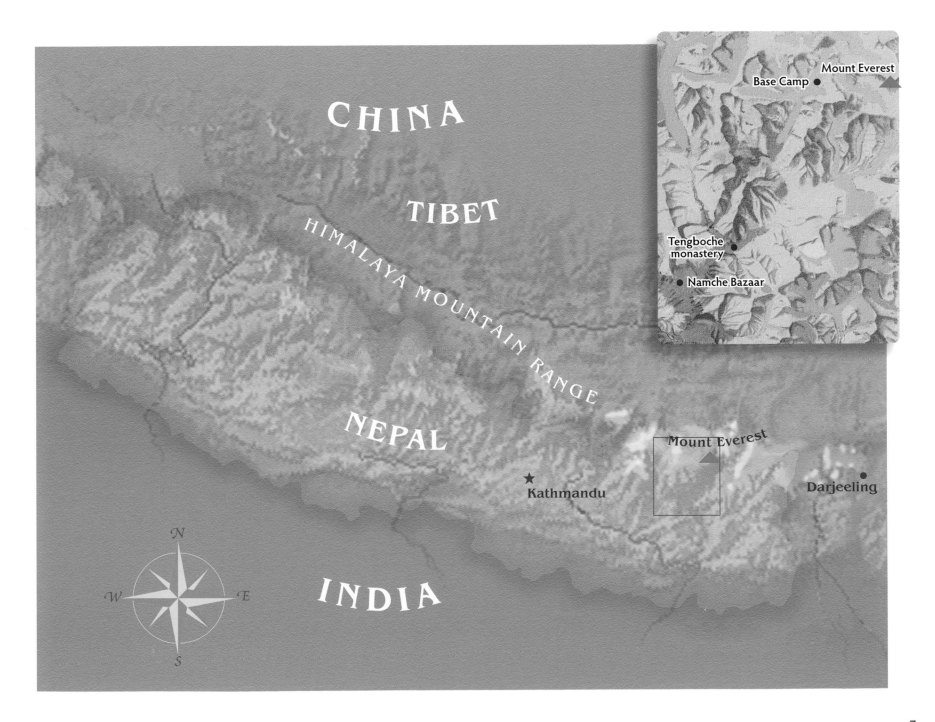

CHINA

TIBET

HIMALAYA MOUNTAIN RANGE

NEPAL

★ Kathmandu

Mount Everest

Darjeeling

INDIA

N
W E
S

Mount Everest

Base Camp ●

Tengboche monastery ●

● Namche Bazaar

TIGERS OF THE SNOW

"The Sherpas have so many characteristics that we, as
Westerners, like to think we have:
They are tough, courteous, tolerant, and cheerful."

—*Sir Edmund Hillary, one of first two men to reach the
summit of Mount Everest*

The Sherpa are descendants of people who migrated to the sacred mountain hundreds of years ago from the Tibetan province of Kham. *Sher* means "east" and *pa* means "people" in the Tibetan language, so *Sherpa* means "People of the East."

More than five hundred years ago, Sherpas began traveling between Nepal and India to trade. They brought salt, wool, dried meat, jewelry, Chinese silks, and porcelain. They traded these goods for grains such as barley, rice, and corn. Sugar and paper from India were also prized by Sherpa traders.

The Sherpa used a trading route called Nangpa La. This glacial passage cuts through the mountains at a height of 19,000 feet (5,791 meters) above sea level. Nangpa La is only safe for travel during a few months each year. At such a high altitude, the temperature is bitter cold and the oxygen level is low. Most people could not survive the trip without help, but Sherpas' bodies were adapted to the thin air and harsh climate. They were able to carry bundles weighing hundreds of pounds for long distances. Today, Sherpas are often called Tigers of the Snow because of their rugged strength and bravery.

Ancient Buddhist legends told of a hidden valley in the mountains that would provide protection, food, and shelter in times of war or famine. Some of the Sherpa traders established a post called Namche Bazaar in the Khumbu valley. The trading post was located at 11,286 feet (3,440 meters). As the legends said, wood and water were plentiful there. The mountain protected the valley from the extreme rains during the summer monsoon season and the heavy snows of the winter season. Other Sherpa traders continued south and built villages in the Solu region. Today, more than three thousand Sherpa live in the upper Khumbu. Thousands more live in towns and villages nearby.

Family Life and Religion

There are more than a dozen Sherpa clans. These are family groups descended from a common ancestor. People do not marry within the same clan. When a daughter weds she receives a dowry—gifts of money, jewelry, rugs, and items for her new house. When a son weds he receives a share of his parents' land and animals. The youngest son inherits the family house and must take care of his parents. Families without a son may adopt their youngest daughter's husband, the *maksu*, as their son.

A Sherpa House

Villages range in size from a dozen houses to more than one hundred. A traditional Sherpa house is built of stone walls coated with white clay. The roof is constructed from heavy timbers weighted down with stones, or from metal, which is more wind resistant. Windows are placed in the south wall to receive maximum sunlight.

Bins of food are stored on the first floor. This area is also used to house livestock. A wooden ladder leads to the living quarters on the second floor. This long room contains a hearth for cooking and heating. The floor is covered with rugs and carpets, and benches or platforms are used for sitting and sleeping. Household items and clothing are stored in trunks and cabinets on the north wall. There is also a small altar for worship. Many Sherpa homes today use hydroelectric power, but some in the upper Khumbu still do not have running water, electricity, or telephones.

When a child is born, parents report the day and time of the birth to their spiritual leader, a high-ranking monk called a *lama*. A naming ceremony and feast are held within five to eleven days. Children are sometimes named for the day of the week on which they were born, so a child born on Saturday might be called Pemba, the Sherpa word for "Saturday."

Sherpa children are raised mostly by their mothers or grandparents. Fathers often work far away from home, on trading expeditions, or tending livestock and crops in the valley. Children help with household chores, fetch water, and gather firewood and animal dung for fuel. They stay home until they are big enough to walk to school, a trip that can take more than two hours each way.

A typical school day is similar to school in North America. Children study English and Nepali, math, social studies, science, religion, and arts and crafts. During recess, they play games or sports. Table tennis, soccer, and jump rope are popular.

Families who can afford tuition send their children to boarding school in Kathmandu, the capital of Nepal. Children whose families cannot afford private school often drop out of school after age ten. These older children watch the younger children and perform household and farming chores so their mothers and fathers can work outside the home or away from the village. At age fifteen, many boys begin doing adult jobs such as mountain trekking or working as porters, carrying heavy loads on climbing expeditions. They often give their full wages to help support their families.

Sherpa Days of the Week

Nyi'ma:	Sunday
Dawa:	Monday
Mingma:	Tuesday
Lhakpa:	Wednesday
Phurba:	Thursday
Pasang:	Friday
Pemba:	Saturday

Children carrying baskets strapped to their heads

Students singing at school

The center of religious life is the village *gomba*, or temple. Monks and lamas conduct religious ceremonies for important life events such as marriage, birth, and death. A ritual worship ceremony called a *puja* is performed for these occasions. Before a man can ask to marry a woman, for example, a puja is held to ask the gods' permission. If the woman accepts the man's proposal, there are four more stages of prayer and activities before the marriage can be performed. The process can take many years.

Monks and lamas live in monasteries throughout the Khumbu region. The most honored lama of a monastery is the *Rinpoche*, which is Tibetan for "precious one." Before climbing a mountain, visitors stop at a monastery to ask the Rinpoche for prayers, blessings, and advice.

The Tengboche monastery is the largest monastery in the Khumbu valley. One legend says that long ago a monk traveled to the valley to meditate. While climbing, he slipped and left a footprint in the rock. He believed it was a sign that the land was the perfect place to build a monastery. Behind the monastery lies a mountain named Khumbila. The Sherpa believe that the god who protects the valley lives on this mountain. Although Sherpas climb Everest, they are forbidden to climb Khumbila.

Boys may enter a monastery at the age of seven. There they are taught to read and write the Nepali and Tibetan languages. They also receive religious training. Some boys study to become monks. Others eventually leave the monastery to take jobs helping mountain climbers and other tourists.

Festivals

Festivals are popular on Mount Everest. *Lhosar*, the Tibetan lunar new year, is celebrated in February at the time of the new moon. For three days people celebrate with feasts, folk songs, and dances. They go to the temples or monasteries for ceremonies and to make offerings to the gods. The first day of Lhosar is spent with family. The next two days are celebrated with friends and visitors.

Mani Rimdu, a ritual blessing of the people, occurs in late October or early November. The exact date is determined according to the lunar calendar. At the beginning of the festival, monks create a sacred painting called a *mandala* using fine grains of colored sand. The

Buddhist monks waiting for the start of
Mani Rimdu

Buddhist monks creating a mandala

colors of the sand represent earth, water, fire, wind, and air; and it takes four days to complete the design. The Sherpa celebrate by praying, dancing, and feasting. After nine days of prayer, the monks perform masked dances called *Cham*. These dances show how Buddhist teachings can help people conquer inner demons such as hatred, vanity, and greed. On the last day of the festival, a puja fire ceremony is held and the mandala is destroyed in a sacred ritual. The sand is scattered to spread the mandala's healing powers to the world.

Masked Cham dancer performing during Mani Rimdu

How the Himalaya Were Formed

More than 250 million years ago, Earth's landmass was a single supercontinent known as Pangaea, surrounded by one ocean.

- Over the next 25 million years, Pangaea broke apart, forming smaller continents that drifted away from one another.
- About 50 million years ago, India collided with the Asian Continental Plate, pushing up Earth's crust.
- During the next 30 million years of intense pressure, sediments were pushed up from deep seabeds on the ocean floor. This formed the base of the Himalaya mountain range.
- About 8 million years ago, a major shift in the continental plates caused the mountain range to rise suddenly. The top of Mount Everest contains fossils of animals and plants that once lived at the bottom of the ocean.
- India continues to move north, pushing underneath Asia. As a result, Everest grows taller by about 0.16 inch (4 millimeters) each year.

PANGAEA

Measuring the Mountain

How do you measure a mountain of such enormous height? It is not easy. In the mid 1800s, when Great Britain ruled India, Nepal and Tibet did not allow visitors. British surveyors had to work from survey stations in India, more than 100 miles (161 kilometers) away, to measure the mountain. They used instruments called theodolites, which weighed more than 1,000 pounds (454 kilograms) each and had to be hoisted up 50-foot (15-meter) towers. Indian mathematician Radhanath Sickdhar studied the data from the survey stations. In 1852, he concluded the mountain was the tallest in the world, rising 29,000 feet (8,840 meters) above sea level. The survey leader, Andrew Waugh, feared such an exact round number would be considered an estimate, so he added 2 feet (0.6 meter) to the height. Waugh also suggested that the mountain be named after Sir George Everest, who had been the surveyor-general of India before him. England's Royal Geographical Society adopted the name Mount Everest in 1865.

Theodolite

In 1984, a team sponsored by the National Geographic Society, Boston's Museum of Science, and the Kingdom of Nepal flew in a Learjet at 40,000 feet (12,192 meters) to shoot aerial photographs of the surface of Everest. The team members combined their photographs with those taken by the United States space shuttle *Columbia* to create a three-dimensional model of the mountain.

In 1999, the Everest Millennium Expedition used Global Positioning System (GPS) software to collect data about Mount Everest from twelve satellites orbiting above Earth. Scientists at the Massachusetts Institute of Technology developed a portable device that could penetrate the snow and find the actual top of the mountain. The United States team determined that Mount Everest was 29,035 feet (8,850 meters) above sea level.

Sir George Everest

17

LIVING IN HARMONY WITH CHOMOLUNGMA

"I feel a family connection to the mountain. I feel it was written on my forehead at birth."

—*Jamling Tenzing Norgay, son of mountaineer Tenzing Norgay*

As Buddhists, the Sherpa believe all life is sacred. They live in harmony with the natural world around them and consider the mountains, lakes, and forests to be the homes of gods and goddesses. The Sherpa believe these spirits affect the weather, the harvest, and the health of all living beings. Even the act of cutting down a tree must be done with care so as not to upset the gods.

Weather and Climate Zones

Mount Everest is divided into four climate zones. Forests filled with birch, juniper, pine, fir, and bamboo are found in the **lower alpine zone**, below 11,483 feet (3,500 meters). Wild rhododendrons grow up to 30 feet (9 meters) tall. That is three times the height of rhododendrons grown in North America. Many native plants found on Everest can be used for food or medicine.

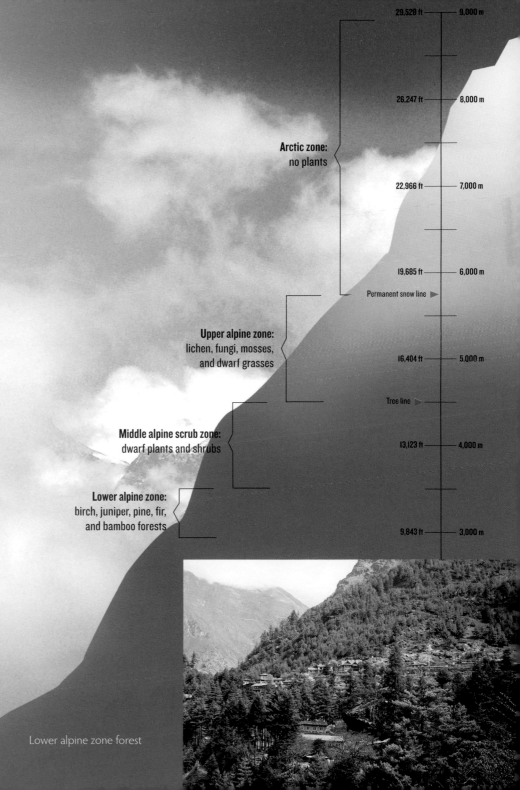

Lower alpine zone in bloom during summer

Forests cover only three percent of the land. Some are considered sacred and protected. A half-human, half-serpent spirit called a *lu* is believed to inhabit these forests. Disturbing the lu could cause misfortune to befall a village.

The **middle alpine scrub zone** is next, and goes up to the tree line at 14,764 feet (4,500 meters). Dwarf plants and shrubs grow in the meadows. The rhododendrons here are not much bigger than small bushes.

During the summer monsoon season, with its heavy rains, both the lower and middle alpine zones burst into bloom with colorful flowers. Eighty percent of the annual rain falls at this time.

The **upper alpine zone** begins at the tree line. It is the highest place on the mountain where plants can be found. Trees and bushes cannot grow at this altitude. Plant life is limited to lichen, fungi, mosses, and dwarf grasses.

The permanent snow line starts at 18,865 feet (5,750 meters) and stretches up to the summit of the mountain. This is the **arctic zone**. The land is bare. No plants can grow in the harsh climate.

Living Off the Land

Sherpa villages are located in the lower alpine zone, where the weather is warmer. During the summer monsoon, villagers move to huts higher up in the valley

Lower alpine zone forest

29,528 ft — 9,000 m

26,247 ft — 8,000 m

Arctic zone: no plants

22,966 ft — 7,000 m

19,685 ft — 6,000 m

Permanent snow line ▶

Upper alpine zone: lichen, fungi, mosses, and dwarf grasses

16,404 ft — 5,000 m

Tree line ▶

Middle alpine scrub zone: dwarf plants and shrubs

13,123 ft — 4,000 m

Lower alpine zone: birch, juniper, pine, fir, and bamboo forests

9,843 ft — 3,000 m

to be close to grazing pastures and crop fields. Until 1949, a village or clan owned and passed on its land under the *kipat* system. In 1950, kipat was eliminated. Families were then allowed to register ownership of their land and to sell it to others or divide it among family members.

Many Sherpas are subsistence farmers. They eat most of what they grow and trade what is left for supplies. Sherpas must grow enough food in summer to last through the long winter. They terrace small plots of land along the steep mountain slopes. To protect grazing and crop land, guardians called *santok nawas* are appointed. These nawas determine when to move livestock to new pastures and when to rotate crop fields so the land remains fertile.

In May, monks or lamas gather with villagers to bless the earth before crops are planted. They all walk in a circle around the outer edges of the fields carrying prayer flags, sacred books, and statues from local gombas. Cymbals, horns, and drums are played while the monks or lamas stick the flagpoles into the earth and recite prayers. Grain may be collected from each family to help pay for the ceremony.

Farmers till the soil by pulling wooden plows across the ground. They then scatter seeds on the soil and drag logs across the fields to push the seeds into the ground. Stone walls surround the plots to keep out grazing animals. A *Dumje* is held in late June or early July at the time of the full moon. During this festival, monks ask the gods to protect the farmers' harvests and scare away evil spirits. Crops are harvested between August and November.

Meals are hearty and filling to help people survive in the cold climate. Potatoes, barley, and buckwheat grow well at high altitudes and are staples of the Sherpa diet. Vegetables are preserved so they will last through the winter. *Dal bhaat*, a stew made from boiled lentils,

Woman preparing rice

Young girl cooking cheese curds

long to prepare the tea, because water boils faster at high altitudes than at sea level. The boiling water is poured into a wooden churn filled with black tea leaves, salt, and yak butter. After brewing for a few minutes, the rich, salty tea is served with yak milk. Barley flour is mixed with the tea to make a thick porridge called *tsampa*.

Domestic Animals

Herding livestock is an important part of Sherpa life. Sherpa families raise yak and *zopkio*. A yak is a large, long-haired ox. Yak are sure-footed on narrow mountain paths. Traders use them to carry heavy bundles at the high altitudes and extreme climate of the mountains. A yak can weigh more than 1,000 pounds (454 kilograms) and grow up to 6 feet (1.8 meters) tall. Yak forage for

spices, and rice, is the most common traditional dish. Some Sherpa families eat this stew twice a day.

Although Buddhism forbids the killing of animals, Sherpas may eat meat if an animal is killed accidentally or is slaughtered by a professional butcher. Yak meat and potatoes are cooked together in a stew called *shyakpa*. *Momos* are small, steamed flour dumplings filled with chopped meat or other ingredients.

Sherpas drink Tibetan tea throughout the day, and visitors to a village or monastery are always offered tea as a sign of welcome and hospitality. It does not take

Riding a yak carrying heavy bundles

food during winter and do not need to be kept in stables. They cannot survive at low altitudes and are rarely seen below 9,800 feet (2,987 meters).

A zopkio is a cross between a yak and a cow. Zopkio serve as pack animals in the lower and middle alpine zones and can be used to pull plows. They cannot survive in the higher altitudes. They must be housed in stables and fed during the winter.

A female yak is called a *nak*, and a female zopkio is called a *zhum*. Nak and zhum are important sources of milk. Sherpa women turn this milk into butter, cheese, and yogurt. Yak dung is used as fertilizer and is dried for use as cooking fuel.

Enjoying a ride on a zopkio

Sherpa Clothing

The Sherpa weave yak and sheep wool into elaborate blankets and cloth from which they make clothing. The oils in yak wool repel water, making the cloth naturally waterproof.

Traditionally, Sherpa men and women wear a *chuba*, a long woolen robe tied with a sash. A woman's chuba is called an *ungi*. Women also wear silk shirts and woolen dresses, and married women wear striped aprons. Turquoise, often worn as jewelry, is considered a symbol of good luck and health. Men wear a *chuwa*, a long shirt that crosses in the front. Both women and men wear woolen boots with soles made of animal hides.

Today many Sherpa wear Western clothing, and some men also wear cowboy hats.

Wildlife

The Sherpa believe all life has value and serves a greater purpose. Wild animals are respected, and there is wildlife found on Mount Everest that does not live anywhere else on Earth.

Most wild animals live in the lower and middle alpine zones. Scientists have counted twenty-eight species of mammals, including the Himalayan tahr, Himalayan black bear, gray wolf, musk deer, and snow leopard. There is even a rare species, the Himalayan red panda.

The Himalayan tahr is a type of wild goat. Tahrs' padded hooves allow them to climb narrow rock ledges. They graze in high pastures during summer and then in winter move lower down the mountain to the forest for protection from the winds. Tahrs sometimes dig up farmers' potato crops with their hooves and damage vegetation on the mountain.

Himalayan black bears are solitary creatures. They

Himalayan tahrs

sleep in caves or in the hollows of trees during the day and forage for food at night. They have long black fur with a crescent of white fur on their chests. Himalayan bears can weigh up to 440 pounds (200 kilograms) and can climb trees to search for food. Scientists believe these bears may be the origin of the Yeti myth.

In 2004, a research scientist photographed a snow leopard on Mount Everest. It was the first time in more than forty years that a leopard had been seen on the mountain. Loss of natural habitat and hunting have

Himalayan red panda

threatened the leopards, but current conservation efforts offer hope for the animals' survival.

Mount Everest is also home to more than one hundred eighteen species of birds, including the brilliantly colored Impeyan pheasant, the national bird of Nepal. This pheasant lives in the forest during winter and travels above the tree line in summer. Impeyan pheasants eat seeds, roots, and tubers. Like the tahr, pheasants can ruin a field of crops while foraging for food. Farmers sometimes plant extra crops to make up for losses to wild animals.

Snow leopard

The Mysterious Yeti

Many people have heard of the Abominable Snowman, a large, apelike animal that walks on two legs. This legendary creature is based on the mythical Yeti believed to live on the glaciers in Nepal and Tibet. *Yeti* means "magical creature," "man bear," or "rock bear."

In 1951, British expedition leader Eric Shipton took photographs of large footprints on Mount Everest that he believed were made by a Yeti. In 1960, Sir Edmund Hillary led a search for a Yeti but could not find one. In 1986, mountaineer Reinhold Messner saw a fur-covered creature that stood on two legs and moved with great speed. It disappeared up the slopes of the mountain.

Scientists think the Yeti may actually be a large bear, an ape, or a monkey. For many years, the Pangboche monastery in the Khumbu valley displayed a skull and hairs the monks believed belonged to a Yeti. The skull was later stolen, so no physical proof exists. Some people say stories about the Yeti were created to frighten away explorers and climbers, thus helping to preserve Mount Everest's natural resources.

REACHING FOR THE SUMMIT

> "I can't understand why men make all this fuss about Everest. It's only a mountain."
>
> —*Junko Tabei, first woman to reach the summit of Mount Everest*

History is filled with stories of men and women from all over the world who have tried to conquer Mount Everest. The earliest climbers did not truly understand the dangers that awaited them.

Before 1920, access to the mountain was limited because Tibet and Nepal did not allow foreigners to cross their borders. Then in 1920, England's Royal Geographical Society and Alpine Club appealed to the 13th Dalai Lama, the Buddhist leader and head of the Tibetan government. In exchange for gifts, the Dalai Lama granted permission for an expedition to climb and survey the mountain from the north.

Because of the high altitude and extreme conditions, the climbers needed help to navigate the route and carry supplies. In 1921, the expedition leaders traveled from Tibet to Darjeeling, in India, where many Sherpa had gone in search of work. There the British hired Sherpas as guides and porters. The journey to India took six weeks in each direction. Upon its return to Tibet, the expedition team visited the Rongbuk monastery, which sits at the base of the Rongbuk Glacier. The Rinpoche warned the climbers that the gods would cause harm to those who did not respect the mountain.

The team, which included British climber George

Mallory, was unable to scale the mountain. Ice, severe winds, and thin air made completing the trip impossible. Mallory tried again in 1922 with another expedition team. This time the climbers took a supply of oxygen, but the oxygen tanks leaked. The team had to turn around at 1 mile (1.6 kilometers) from the top. Determined, Mallory tried a third time. On this trip the climbers triggered an avalanche. Seven Sherpas were swept away in the snow. Consumed with guilt and grief, Mallory returned to England.

The British team returned in 1924. The climbers reached 28,128 feet (8,573 meters) before exhaustion and bitter cold weather forced them to turn back. Equipped with crude oxygen equipment and ordinary winter clothing, George Mallory set out to climb the north face of the mountain one last time. He and his climbing partner, Andrew Irvine, never returned. No one knows if they reached the summit.

Thirteen people died trying to climb Everest in 1924. The Dalai Lama believed the climbers had upset the gods and goddesses of the mountain. He stopped exploration. Then in 1931, to restore friendly relations with the British, the Dalai Lama granted permission for expeditions to return. Teams climbed the mountain in 1933, 1935, 1936, and 1938. Severe weather or illness forced the climbers to abandon each attempt. Except for the 1933 attempt, all these expeditions included a young porter, Tenzing Norgay.

In 1950, China invaded Tibet and closed the northern route to Everest. The Kingdom of Nepal then opened its borders to allow climbers to approach the mountain from the south. The government issued only one permit each year. Teams wanting to explore the mountain had to wait their turn.

England's Royal Geographical Society sponsored an expedition led by Eric Shipton in 1951. Tenzing Norgay joined them. The team climbed as far as the Khumbu

George Mallory, left, and Andrew Irvine at camp,
preparing for their climb

Icefall, a steep and dangerous area of the Khumbu Glacier resembling a frozen waterfall. A deep cavity in the ice prevented them from crossing the icefall. A second attempt failed due to severe weather.

The British wanted to try again in 1952, but that year the permit was granted to the Swiss. Expedition leader Raymond Lambert hired Tenzing Norgay as a full climbing member. Norgay tried to find other Sherpas to join the expedition as porters, but many refused because the British had treated them so badly the year before. Norgay finally found thirteen Sherpa men who agreed to join the team because the Swiss provided better pay and equipment than the British had.

The team stopped at the Tengboche monastery, where the Rinpoche offered them Tibetan butter tea. Most of the Swiss climbers refused to drink it. Lambert drank his cup, and then drank everyone else's tea as well. Norgay and Lambert soon became friends.

Twice the Swiss team climbed the mountain, and twice the climbers failed to reach the summit. On the first climb, Norgay and Lambert crossed the Khumbu Icefall and got within 700 feet (213 meters) of the mountaintop. But it was getting late. The climbers knew that if they did not turn around, they would not make it back to camp alive in the dark.

Knowing the British held the permit for 1953, the Swiss team made a second climb in the fall. No team had ever attempted a climb so late in the year. The weather proved to be too dangerous. An avalanche trapped twelve climbers and knocked one Sherpa unconscious. The Swiss reluctantly abandoned the expedition.

The British now had another chance to reach the top of Everest. Colonel John Hunt replaced Shipton as the expedition leader. Hunt's team included a New Zealander, beekeeper and mountain climber Edmund Hillary. The team had spent the previous year planning everything from food, clothing, and climbing supplies to the placement of camping sites along the route to the summit. New oxygen canisters were designed for the trip. Hunt hired Tenzing Norgay and other Sherpas to accompany the team. The British treated the Sherpa guides as servants, forcing them to sleep in a stable without sleeping bags or bathroom facilities before setting off for the mountain. The behavior of the British team offended the Sherpa guides. The British climbers believed they did not need the Sherpas' help once the expedition crossed the Khumbu Icefall.

Edmund Hillary, left, and Tenzing Norgay near the summit of Mount Everest, May 1953

While traveling back to Base Camp from a higher camp, Hillary reached an opening in the glacier, an area named The Atom Bomb. Hillary leaped over the opening, but the ice broke and he tumbled into the cavity. Norgay drove his ax into the snow, wrapped Hillary's rope around

it, and pulled him out. Norgay's quick thinking saved Hillary's life. Hillary realized the team needed Norgay's skills and experience, and those of the other Sherpas, for the expedition to succeed.

On May 26, two of the British climbers stopped 300 feet (91 meters) from the summit because one of their oxygen canisters wasn't working properly. Two days later, Norgay and Hillary set out for the summit. They dug out a campsite on a cold, narrow ledge and slept until four in the morning. Hillary had to thaw his frozen boots for two hours before he could put them on. Finally, as the sun rose, the two men started toward the summit ridge.

At eleven-thirty that morning, May 29, 1953, Tenzing Norgay and Edmund Hillary made history. They became the first humans known to have set foot on the highest point on Earth.

Edmund Hillary, left, and Tenzing Norgay after their successful
climb to the summit, 1953

Not Without Risk

The success of Norgay and Hillary excited the imaginations of people around the world. Thousands flocked to the area with dreams of reaching the top of Mount Everest. Tourism became a major part of the mountain economy. To take advantage of Everest's popularity, China reopened the northern route to the mountain in 1979.

This increased access worried the Sherpa. Everest became a tourist attraction open to any climber with enough money to pay fees as high as U.S. $100,000 per person. Sometimes people who had little climbing experience and whose bodies were not conditioned or strong enough to survive in the brutal environment attempted to reach the summit. This endangered everyone on the expeditions.

Climbing the mountain involves huge risks. The weather is unpredictable and can change at any moment. Spring is considered the safest time to climb. The weather is warmer then, and there is less rain and snow. Climbers often arrive at Base Camp as early as March but have only the months of April and May to make their attempts to reach the summit. Four camps are placed along the southern route. Five are placed along the northern route.

Southern route to the summit of Mount Everest

Once on the mountain, climbers must stay at each camp long enough for their bodies to adjust to the altitude. This can take from a few days to a few weeks. Climbers sometimes stay at higher elevations and then come down for a while to help their bodies grow stronger.

The temperature drops quickly at higher altitudes. Even experienced climbers can get frostbite or suffer from hypothermia, a condition in which the body's temperature falls too low. Deep cracks in the ice, called crevasses, are a hidden danger. Sudden snowstorms can make it impossible for climbers to find their way back to camp. An avalanche can occur without warning, burying

Sherpas carrying heavy gear on the Khumbu Icefall

everything in its path and totally changing the landscape.

The area above 25,000 feet (7,620 meters) is called the Death Zone. Temperatures can fall to -100 degrees Fahrenheit (-73 degrees Celsius). Wind speeds as high as 100 miles (161 kilometers) per hour have been reported. Altitude sickness and lack of oxygen are two of the most dangerous threats. The air contains only one-third the amount of oxygen found at sea level. Most climbers are not able to survive in these conditions without special clothing and equipment.

It can take as long as two months to reach the summit of Everest. Much of this time is spent getting used to the altitude and waiting for ideal weather. On the final approach up the mountain, climbers must reach the top by noon and can stay there only a few minutes before returning to camp. By then the climbers are exhausted and have used up most of their oxygen. If they delay, the climbers also risk navigating the dangerous ice and rocks in the dark. Those who do not reach the summit early in the day must often wait a full year or more before trying again.

Crossing a Glacier

Glaciers, huge sheets of ice up to 3 miles (4.8 kilometers) long, cover the Himalaya. Gravity pulls the sheets of ice slowly down the mountains. Scientists estimate that one-fifth of the world's freshwater is frozen in these glaciers.

The Khumbu Glacier is 18,000 feet (5,486 meters) above sea level. People who climb the south face of Mount Everest stop at a Base Camp below the glacier. They stay there for several days or weeks to adapt to the altitude before climbing farther up the mountain. When they set out, climbers must cross the Khumbu Icefall. The icefall moves slowly, but crevasses can open up without warning. If the crevasses are hidden by snow, a climber walking there could fall through. Blocks of ice, from the size of a car to a large house, can also break away from the icefall, instantly crushing anything and anyone below. Many people have died attempting to navigate the Khumbu Icefall.

Climbers at the top of Mount Everest, prayer flags flapping in the strong winds, 1998

More Mount Everest Firsts

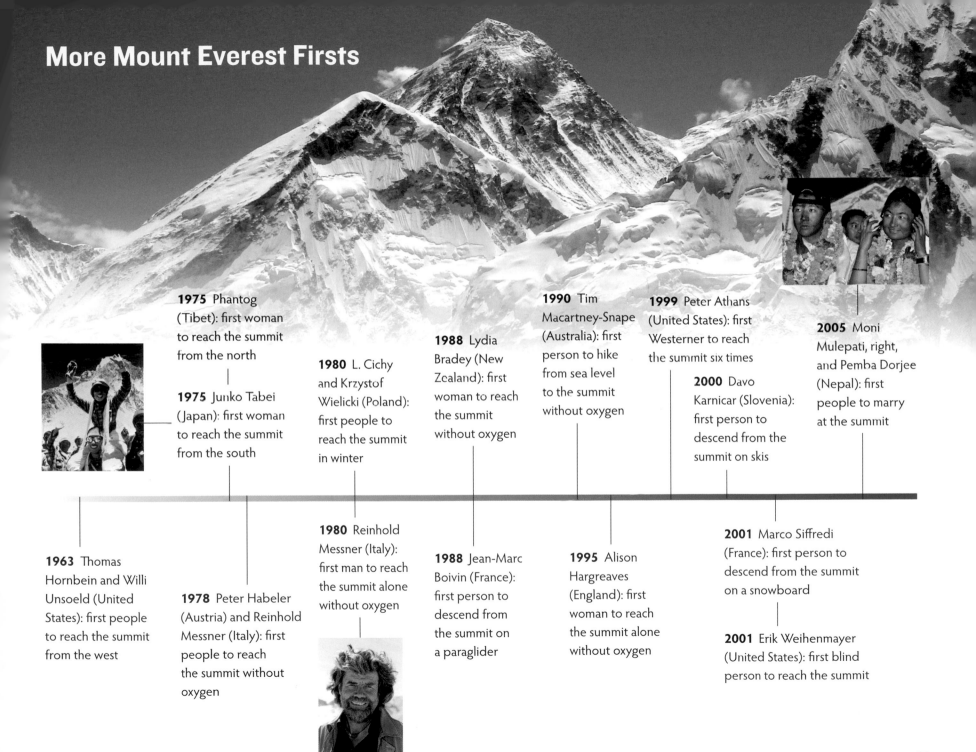

1975 Phantog (Tibet): first woman to reach the summit from the north

1975 Junko Tabei (Japan): first woman to reach the summit from the south

1980 L. Cichy and Krzystof Wielicki (Poland): first people to reach the summit in winter

1988 Lydia Bradey (New Zealand): first woman to reach the summit without oxygen

1990 Tim Macartney-Snape (Australia): first person to hike from sea level to the summit without oxygen

1999 Peter Athans (United States): first Westerner to reach the summit six times

2000 Davo Karnicar (Slovenia): first person to descend from the summit on skis

2005 Moni Mulepati, right, and Pemba Dorjee (Nepal): first people to marry at the summit

1963 Thomas Hornbein and Willi Unsoeld (United States): first people to reach the summit from the west

1978 Peter Habeler (Austria) and Reinhold Messner (Italy): first people to reach the summit without oxygen

1980 Reinhold Messner (Italy): first man to reach the summit alone without oxygen

1988 Jean-Marc Boivin (France): first person to descend from the summit on a paraglider

1995 Alison Hargreaves (England): first woman to reach the summit alone without oxygen

2001 Marco Siffredi (France): first person to descend from the summit on a snowboard

2001 Erik Weihenmayer (United States): first blind person to reach the summit

33

RECLAIMING THE MOUNTAIN

*"When a Sherpa climbs Everest . . . for us,
it is a journey into the lap of God."*

—*Norbu Tenzing Norgay, son of mountaineer
Tenzing Norgay*

Sherpa climber on Mount Everest

While foreigners receive the world's attention when they climb Mount Everest, the accomplishments of the Sherpa have often been overlooked. Sherpa guides blaze the trails, set up camps, and carry most of the supplies. This often means crossing the Khumbu Icefall multiple times with heavy loads to get all the equipment to the other side. Because Sherpas are accustomed to the high altitudes, some reach the summit before their teammates. It is nearly impossible for most climbers to survive the journey up the mountain without the help of Sherpa guides and porters.

For Tenzing Norgay, climbing the mountain was a dangerous way to make a living. But like many Sherpa, he felt it was the best way. The money he earned helped him provide for his children's education and a future free from poverty.

As tourism grew, more and more world attention was focused on climbers who reached Everest's summit. The Sherpa believed it was time for them to reclaim the sacred mountain they call Chomolungma as their own.

Tenzing Norgay

Tenzing Norgay was born Namgyal Wangdi in 1914, the eleventh of fourteen children. He suffered from ill health, so his parents took him to a popular Rinpoche, Nawang Tenzin Norbu, for a renaming ceremony. Tibetans believe this practice gives a child a new start in life.

The Rinpoche revealed that Namgyal was the reincarnation of a wealthy man who had recently died. Namgyal was given the new name Tenzing Norgay, which means "wealthy follower of religion."

As a boy, Tenzing was sent to a monastery to become a monk, but he ran away and returned home. Tenzing tended yak for his family and dreamed of joining a mountain-climbing expedition. In 1933, he moved to India, hoping to join the British climbing team. He had no experience and was turned down. Two years later, the expedition led by Eric Shipton needed last-minute replacements. Tenzing Norgay was one of two porters selected. Thus, his climbing career began.

In Italy, 1958

After reaching the summit of Mount Everest with Edmund Hillary in 1953, Norgay became a celebrity. He traveled all over the world to bring attention to his people and their culture. He never learned to read or write, but he spoke ten languages. For twenty-two years, Norgay was Director of Field Training for the Himalayan Mountaineering Institute. The institute teaches others how to climb safely and with respect for the mountains. Tenzing Norgay died in 1986, but his legacy lives on through his family.

On the summit of Mount Everest, 1953

The Men

In 1991, the Sherpa Everest Expedition consisting of Nepali climbers Apa Sherpa, Ang Temba, and Sonam Dendu reached the summit of the mountain. Apa Sherpa and Lhakpa Gelu Sherpa later joined forces to create SuperSherpas Expeditions. Their goals were to bring attention to the Nepali people and to fund educational opportunities for the children of Nepal. Their climbs also help educate the world about the accomplishments of the Sherpa.

As of 2008, Apa Sherpa held the world record for reaching the summit of Mount Everest eighteen times. Lhakpa Gelu Sherpa had climbed to the summit thirteen times. He held the world record for the fastest climb—10 hours, 56 minutes, 46 seconds—until Pemba Dorji Sherpa broke it in 2004. He reached the top of the mountain in 8 hours, 10 minutes.

Ang Rita Sherpa has reached the summit ten times without oxygen, which earned him the name Snow Leopard. He has climbed the world's other highest mountains as well. Babu Chhiri Sherpa climbed Mount Everest ten times and once stayed on the summit for twenty-one hours without oxygen.

The Women

In 1993, Pasang Lhamu Sherpa became the first Nepali woman to reach the summit. Although she died in a storm on the way down, her climb was an important milestone. In traditional Sherpa culture, women do not receive much schooling. They do not lead climbs or guide others up the mountain. Pasang Lhamu Sherpa was a trailblazer who defied tradition and became a symbol of hope and opportunity for women. After her death, the king of Nepal awarded her the Nepal Star, a medal for outstanding merit. A statue was also erected in her honor.

In 2000, the first all-female Sherpa team climbed the mountain. The Nepalese Women Millennium Everest Expedition included Lhakpa Sherpa, Dawa Yangzi Sherpa, Mingma Yangzi Sherpa, Kesang Dikki Sherpa, and Dolma Sherpa. At 23,000 feet (7,010 meters), Mingma had a nightmare about death and decided to turn around. At 28,000 feet (8,534 meters), Dawa, the

Apa Sherpa, left, and Lhakpa Gelu Sherpa at the summit, May 2007

youngest member, felt ill and returned to camp. Lhakpa Sherpa climbed the final 1,000 feet (305 meters) to the summit alone. That same year, Pemba Doma Sherpa became the first Nepali woman to reach the top of the mountain from Tibet. In 2002, she led the Nepalese Woman Everest Expedition to bring awareness of Nepali women to the world.

Lhakpa Sherpa continued to climb the mountain. In 2003, she became the only woman to reach the summit of Everest three times. That year her fifteen-year-old sister, Ming Kipa Sherpa, joined the expedition. Ming became the youngest girl to reach the top of the mountain.

In 2008, ten women from a range of Nepali social classes and ethnic groups set out for the summit. The First Inclusive Women Sagarmatha Expedition (FIWSE) was organized to bring attention to climate change in the Himalaya. All ten team members reached the summit, making this the most successful female expedition to conquer Mount Everest. The climbers hoped their accomplishment would encourage women from different backgrounds to work together to achieve common goals.

The mountain is once again the land of the Sherpa.

Nepalese Women Millennium Everest Expedition 2000; left to right: Kesang Dikki Sherpa, Dawa Yangzi Sherpa, Mingma Yangzi Sherpa (deputy team leader), Lhakpa Sherpa (team leader), and Dolma Sherpa

A MOUNTAIN AT RISK

"Tourism is not only the goose that lays golden eggs . . . it also fouls its own nest."

—*Dr. Kamal Kumar Shrestha, Nepali chemist*

While the introduction of climbing to Mount Everest opened up economic opportunities for the people who live in the surrounding areas, it has also put the mountain in danger. Only a few hundred people are granted permits to climb the mountain each year, but thousands more visit the Khumbu region. Tourists now outnumber Sherpas nine to one. Mount Everest's popularity comes with a terrible price. Tourism has created pollution and damaged the fragile ecosystem.

Deforestation

Wood is the chief source of fuel and building material for the region. A typical Sherpa hearth burns 2.5 tons (2.3 metric tons) of firewood each year. As visitors have flooded the mountain, energy needs have increased. On the south side of Mount Everest, in Nepal, many trees have been cut down to meet the increased demand for homes, lodges, and fuel.

Tourism has also brought money into the area. Sherpa families have used their new income to buy more livestock, a sign of wealth. The additional livestock have led to a reduction of shrubs and plants in the scarce grazing pastures. Trees have been burned to clear land for farming. Before 1950, the Khumbu forests were thick and lush. Now many are almost gone. The loss of trees has reduced animal habitats and caused soil erosion.

In Tibet the problem of deforestation is not as severe. However, increased building in towns and cities below the mountain has meant more demand for lumber. If the demand continues, forests on the north side of Everest may start to disappear as well. That could lead to a loss of habitats for native animals and the extinction of rare plants.

Taking More Than Photographs, Leaving More Than Footprints

Before climbing the mountain, Sherpas and visitors hold a puja to ask permission to enter the sacred home of the gods and goddesses of Everest. They understand that the mountain is to be revered and respected. Once on the mountain, that understanding sometimes changes among the visitors. Climbers focus on their own health and safety. Exhausted from the journey to and from the summit, climbers often leave trash and equipment behind. As a result, the public areas of Everest now look like giant garbage dumps. Empty oxygen canisters, batteries, fuel tanks, bottles, and food waste litter the mountainside, spoiling the landscape.

Because there are no flush toilets, human waste has leaked into the mountain water supply and contaminated it. Visitors have left more than 50 tons (45 metric tons)

Secret Hidden Valleys

A *beyul* is a secret land or valley hidden from all but the faithful. Buddhists believe there are more than one hundred beyul in the Himalaya mountain range. Khumbu is one such region. Although it is no longer a secret, it is a place of beauty that attracts many tourists.

Rafting on the Bhote Kosi

Two deep rivers—the Dudh Kosi and the Bhote Kosi—run south through the Khumbu valley. *Dudh Kosi* means "milky white river." It gets its name from the milky white sediment that washes down the mountain with the water from melting glaciers. The current is very strong and boulders cover the riverbed, so the river cannot be used for boating.

Bhote Kosi means "river from Tibet." Its strong currents make the river popular for white-water rafting. Some adventurers compare traveling over its thundering rapids to riding a roller coaster.

of trash on the mountain since Nepal opened the area to foreigners in 1950.

Many people are troubled by the pollution and the disrespect it shows to the native peoples and their gods. In 1994, expeditions were organized to clean up the mountain. More than 2,200 pounds (998 kilograms) of garbage were removed that year. Since then, several more clean-up expeditions have been organized. A treatment plant was built to handle human waste. Glass bottles have been banned from the mountain.

The government of Nepal now requires climbers to pay a U.S. $4,000 environmental security deposit before climbing. The money is not returned unless the climbers bring all their trash back with them. The Nepal Mountaineering Association offers specific guidelines for safe and respectful handling of equipment and waste on the mountain.

Pollution and Climate Change

Towns and cities in the Mount Everest area are becoming more modern. Airstrips and roads allow planes, cars, buses, and other vehicles to bring people to the mountain by the thousands. In April 2008, China completed a 67-mile (108-kilometer) blacktop road to Base Camp on Everest's north side. The road was built

Chinese climbers carrying Olympic torch to the top of Mount Everest, May 2008

to help runners carry an Olympic torch to the summit in advance of the 2008 Beijing Summer Olympics. The construction of this road brought more vehicles, and more visitors, to the fragile mountain landscape. Carbon dioxide given off by all these vehicles contributes to air pollution on the mountain.

In April 2007, the United Nations Educational, Scientific, and Cultural Organization (UNESCO) reported that global changes in climate have threatened the habitats of many rare animals in the area. Temperatures are rising. Weather patterns are changing. Monsoon rains are heavier and unpredictable. Snowfalls are being

Water from melting glaciers on Mount Everest

reported during spring months, increasing the risk of avalanches and rock slides. Places that normally receive snow are often dry.

The higher temperatures are causing glaciers on the Himalaya mountain range to melt. The water flows into rivers and lakes. If this continues, the rivers and lakes will overflow and nearby villages will be flooded.

The Khumbu Glacier has retreated almost 3 miles (5 kilometers) since 1953. The ice towers of the Rongbuk Glacier on the north side of Mount Everest are also shrinking. They are now half the size they were when climbers first saw them in 1921. Scientists predict that all the glaciers along the Himalaya range will disappear in fifty years if the climate continues to warm at today's rate.

HOPE FOR THE FUTURE

> "I came here for the mountain. I stay for the people. I never want to give that up."
>
> —*Sir Edmund Hillary*

Queen Elizabeth II of Great Britain knighted Edmund Hillary in 1953, shortly after his Everest expedition arrived in London. After this first climb, Hillary returned to Everest many times.

Himalayan Trust

To show his thanks to the Sherpa people and to honor his climbing partner, Tenzing Norgay, Hillary created the Himalayan Trust in 1960. The trust helps improve the lives of the Sherpa.

Although Sherpa communities lacked basic modern facilities, the people's greatest wish was to have schools for their children. The trust has built more than thirty schools since 1960. School supplies are provided free. Scholarships are available to help young women and men attend college. The trust has also built two hospitals and several health clinics to provide free health and dental care.

Using donations from supporters all over the world, the trust is raising awareness about Sherpa culture. Historic sites and buildings are being restored. The

Entrance to Sagarmatha National Park

Lukla airstrip was built so supplies could be flown to the restoration sites. To help replace dwindling forests, thousands of seedlings are planted in nurseries each year. More than one million young trees have been planted on twenty-five protected sites.

Sir Edmund Hillary died on January 10, 2008, but his contributions continue to help the people and mountain he loved.

Sagarmatha National Park

Sagarmatha National Park was established in 1976 to protect the fragile ecosystem from damage by tourism and deforestation. The park covers the upper two-thirds of Mount Everest in Nepal, a total of 450 square miles (1,165 square kilometers). The park starts at 9,335 feet (2,845 meters) above sea level and extends all the way to the summit of the mountain. The northern boundary follows the border between Nepal and Tibet.

Sherpas have been trained to serve as park rangers. Domestic goats are banned from the park to keep them from eating the vegetation. To reduce the dependence on wood, local people are encouraged to burn kerosene for fuel. Visitors to the park must provide their own fuel and are forbidden to burn firewood when camping. Hydroelectric power plants were built. Melted water from the glaciers is used to turn the turbines.

Sherpa villages inside the park appoint *shinga nawas*, forest guardians, who are responsible for controlling the use of forest and wildlife resources. The nawas limit the number of trees that can be cut down, protect vegetation, and report wildlife poaching. Only the six main beams of a Sherpa house may be made of wood from Khumbu forests. The rest must come from outside the region. Nawas collect penalties and fines for violations, and the money must be used for the community. Now that the land is protected and habitats are being reestablished, native animal populations are increasing.

In 1979, Sagarmatha National Park was added to the list of UNESCO World Heritage Sites.

Tenzing Norgay's Legacy

Jamling Tenzing Norgay

To honor his father's memory, Jamling Tenzing Norgay, one of Tenzing Norgay's sons, first climbed to the top of Mount Everest in 1996 while guiding the IMAX Everest Expedition. He wrote a book about his journey called *Touching My Father's Soul*. Today Jamling is a motivational speaker and works for the trekking company his father founded.

Tenzing Norgay's oldest son, Norbu Tenzing Norgay, is vice president of the American Himalayan Foundation. The foundation raises money for education and for cultural and resource preservation for the people of the Himalaya region. He is the narrator of the audiobook edition of his brother's book.

Tashi Tenzing, one of Tenzing Norgay's grandsons, has reached the summit of Everest several times. He started his own trekking company and wrote a book about his grandfather, *Tenzing Norgay and the Sherpas of Everest*.

Norbu Tenzing Norgay

American Himalayan Foundation

For more than twenty-five years, the American Himalayan Foundation (AHF) has been dedicated to helping improve the lives of more than 15,000 people each year. The foundation builds housing, clean-water systems, and bridges. It provides food for the poor and elderly. Parents who work in the fields can send their young children to AHF day care centers, and more than 4,000 children have attended schools established by the foundation. Most go on to college. An orphanage cares for children who have lost their parents. The foundation also trains doctors and helped establish a hospital for disabled children.

The American Himalayan Foundation teamed with the Snow Leopard Conservancy to help villagers build fences and corrals to protect their livestock. The foundation's work with the International Wildlife Conservation Society restores water sources for area wildlife. In partnership with the Himalayan Trust, the AHF also works to establish health and dental clinics, plant forests, and restore historic sites, including the Tengboche monastery. The monastery was rebuilt and dedicated with a ceremony in 1993 after it had burned to the ground in a serious fire in 1989.

When people think of Everest, they most often think of its enormous height and the challenge of reaching the summit. But Everest is more than a mountain carved of rock and ice. It is Chomolungma and Sagarmatha—home to the Sherpa who have served as its spiritual caretakers for hundreds of years. These people and their culture are the mountain's most important legacy, its hope for the future, and its most precious gift to the world.

Glossary and Pronunciation Guide

The spelling and pronunciation of some words spoken in Nepal and Tibet differ depending upon the region. The pronunciations provided here reflect those used by Sherpa-speaking people interviewed by the author or heard on recorded interviews and audiobooks.

beyul (bay-YOOL): secret hidden land or valley

Bhote Kosi (BOAT-eh KOH-zee): river in Nepal with strong currents

Buddhism (BOO-dih-zum): religion based on the teachings of Buddha; developed in India and later spread to China, Japan, Nepal, Tibet, and parts of Southeast Asia

Buddhist (BOO-dist): person who follows the beliefs and practices of Buddhism

Cham (chahm): masked dance that demonstrates Buddhist teachings

Chomolungma (choh-moh-LUNG-muh): Tibetan name for Mount Everest

chuba (CHOO-bah): traditional Sherpa robe

chuwa (CHOO-wah): traditional Sherpa man's shirt

crevasse (kruh-VASS): deep crack in a glacier

Dalai Lama (DAH-lie LAH-muh): Buddhist leader of Tibet

dal bhaat (dahl baht): stew made of lentils and rice

Darjeeling (dahr-JEE-ling): town in northern India where tea is grown; many Sherpa settled there in the early 1920s

Dawa (DAH-wah): Monday

dowry (DOW-ree): gifts a woman brings with her upon marriage

Dudh Kosi (doot KOH-zee): river in Nepal with milky white sediment

Dumje (DOOM-jee): summer festival during which gods are asked to protect the harvest

forage (FOR-ij): to hunt or search for food

glacier (GLAY-shur): large mass of very slowly moving ice

gomba (GAHM-bah): Sherpa village temple

Himalaya (him-uh-LAY-uh): massive mountain range in south-central Asia; includes Mount Everest on the border between Nepal and Tibet

hydroelectric (HI-droh-eh-LEK-trik): production of electricity from waterpower

icefall (ICE-fahl): jumbled mass of ice on a glacier; frozen waterfall

Kathmandu (kat-man-DOO): capital city of Nepal

Khumbila (koom-BIH-lah): mountain near Mount Everest

Khumbu (KOOM-boo): region in Nepal where many Sherpa live

kipat (KEE-pat): system in which land is owned by a community

lama (LAH-muh): high-ranking Buddhist monk

Lhakpa (LAHK-puh): Wednesday

Lhosar (LOH-sahr): Tibetan lunar new year

livestock (LIVE-stok): animals kept or raised for use by people, especially farmers

lu (lew): spirit believed to live in forests

Lukla (LOOK-lah): village in the Khumbu region where an airstrip is located

maksu (MAK-soo): youngest daughter's husband

mandala (MAHN-duh-lah): sacred sand painting

Mani Rimdu (MAH-nee RIM-doo): ritual blessing of the people; festival held after the October full moon

Mingma (MING-mah): Tuesday

Miyolangsangma (MEE-oh-lung-SUNG-mah): Tibetan goddess who lives on Mount Everest

momo (moh-moh): meat-filled dumpling

monastery (MAHN-us-TEH-ree): residence or temple where monks live and work

monk (muhnk): man who is a member of a religious order

monsoon (mahn-SOON): season of heavy rains, usually in summer

nak (nack): female yak

Namche Bazaar (NAHM-chay buh-ZAHR): town and trading post in the Khumbu region; today usually the first stop on a Mount Everest expedition

Nangpa La (NANG-puh lah): high mountain pass between Tibet and Nepal

Nyi'ma (NYEE-muh): Sunday

Pangaea (pan-JEE-uh): giant landmass on Earth believed to have broken up into the present-day continents

Pangboche (PANG-boh-chay): Buddhist monastery on the Nepal side of Mount Everest

Pasang (pah-SAHNG): Friday

Pemba (PEM-buh): Saturday

Phurba (FUR-wuh): Thursday

puja (POOH-jah): ritual worship ceremony; offering

Rinpoche (RIN-poh-chay): highest, most honored lama at a monastery

Rongbuk (RAHNG-book): Buddhist monastery on the Tibet side of Mount Everest

Sagarmatha (sah-gahr-MATH-uh): Nepali name for Mount Everest

santok nawa (SAHN-tuk NAH-wah): Sherpa guardian who protects grazing and crop land

Sherpa (SHUR-puh *or* SHAR-wah): *pl.* people who traveled from Tibet to Nepal and settled in the lower regions of Mount Everest; *s.* language spoken by the Sherpa; surname used by many Sherpa; native person employed for a climbing expedition

shinga nawa (SHING-guh NAH-wah): Sherpa guardian of the forests

shyakpa (shee-AHK-puh): stew made of yak meat and potatoes

surveyor (sir-VAY-uhr): person who measures and records the physical features of land

tahr (tahr): Himalayan wild goat

Tengboche (TANG-boh-chay): Buddhist monastery on the Nepal side of Mount Everest

theodolite (thee-OH-duh-lite): rotating instrument used for measuring height and angles

tsampa (SAM-puh): thick porridge made of tea and barley flour

ungi (OON-jee): traditional Sherpa woman's robe

yak (yack): large, long-haired, domesticated ox

Yeti (YEH-tee): mythical apelike creature believed to live in the Himalaya

zhum (zoom): female zopkio

zopkio (ZOPE-kee-oh): large domestic pack animal that is a cross between a yak and a cow

Acknowledgments

The author would like to thank the creative team at Color-Bridge Books in Brooklyn, New York (Bernette, Diana, Eileen, and Paul, through whom all things are possible), for bringing a beautiful story to life. Special thanks to Jerry Mika of SuperSherpas® for his expertise, his vast photo library, and his encouragement; and to Apa, who currently holds the record for the most climbs (eighteen) to the summit of Mount Everest.

The publisher wishes to thank Peter Athans, The North Face Athlete and first Western climber to summit Mount Everest seven times, for carefully reviewing the manuscript for accuracy.

All illustrations, maps, and charts were created by Paul Colin, Cezanne Studio, New York, New York.

Author's Sources

Breashears, David F. "The Siren Song of Everest." *National Geographic*, September 1997, 124–135.

Carrier, Jim. "Gatekeepers of the Himalaya: Nepal's Sherpa people prosper amid dizzying change as climbers and trekkers descend upon their mountain." *National Geographic*, December 1992, 70–89.

Coburn, Broughton. *Everest: Mountain Without Mercy.* Washington, D.C.: National Geographic Society, 1997.

Douglas, Ed. *Tenzing, Hero of Everest: A Biography of Tenzing Norgay.* Washington, D.C.: National Geographic Society, 2003.

Neale, Jonathan. *Tigers of the Snow: How One Fateful Climb Made the Sherpas Mountaineering Legends.* New York: St. Martin's Press, 2002.

Norgay, Jamling Tenzing. *Touching My Father's Soul: A Sherpa's Journey to the Top of Everest.* San Francisco: HarperCollins, 2001.

Reid, T. R. "The Sherpas: It's their mountain and ever since tourists started pouring in, it's their livelihood too." National Geographic.com: www.ngm.nationalgeographic.com/ngm/0305/feature2/

"Sherpa: Jamling Tenzing Norgay." NPR: Fresh Air from WHHY, May 17, 2002: www.npr.org/templates/story/story.php?storyid=1143508

"Sights and Sounds from Everest: The Sherpas and Edmund Hillary." National Geographic.com: www.ngm.nationalgeographic.com/ngm/0305/sights_n_sounds/media2.html

Venables, Steven. *Everest: Summit of Achievement.* New York: Royal Geographical Society, Simon & Schuster, 2003.

Find Out More About Mount Everest and the Sherpa

American Himalayan Foundation
  www.himalayan-foundation.org
Center for Asian American Media
  www.distribution.asianamericanmedia.org/browse/film/?i=51
Daughters of Everest
  www.therake.com/daughters/proj_desc.html
Discovery Channel (includes an interactive climbing game)
  www.discoverychannel.co.uk/everest/_home/index.shtml
Everest Film Company
  www.everestfilm.com
Frontline: The Legacy of Sherpa Women Mountaineers
  www.pbs.org/frontlineworld/stories/nepal/thestory.html
Nova Online Adventure: Expedition '96: Everest Quest
  www.pbs.org/wgbh/nova/everest/expeditions/96/
SuperSherpas
  www.supersherpas.com
Tengboche Monastery
  www.tengboche.org
Tenzing Norgay Adventures
  www.tenzing-norgay.com

Photograph Credits